HOW TO BECOME WEALTHY FAST

Your Guide To Wealth And Success

Spencer Ryan Maxwell

Table of Contents

INTRODUCTION 4
   DEFINING WEALTH AND SUCCESS 4
CHAPTER ONE 7
   SETTING THE FOUNDATION 7
   SETTING CLEAR FINANCIAL GOALS 14
   EDUCATION AND KNOWLEDGE 23
CHAPTER TWO 32
   INCOME GENERATION 32
   HIGH-INCOME SKILLS AND CAREERS 32
   ENTREPRENEURSHIP 42
   SIDE HUSTLES AND GIG ECONOMY 52
CHAPTER THREE 62
   SMART INVESTING 62
   STOCK MARKET INVESTMENTS 62
   REAL ESTATE INVESTING 71
   CRYPTOCURRENCY AND DIGITAL ASSETS 80
   ALTERNATIVE INVESTMENTS 91
CHAPTER FOUR 100
   FINANCIAL MANAGEMENT 100
   BUDGETING AND SAVING 100
   DEBT MANAGEMENT 107
   TAX OPTIMIZATION 116
CHAPTER FIVE 125
   NETWORKING AND MENTORSHIP 125

- BUILDING A WEALTH NETWORK 125
- MENTORSHIP AND COACHING 132

CHAPTER SIX 143
- SCALING AND SUSTAINING WEALTH 143
- AUTOMATION AND DELEGATION 143
- SUSTAINING WEALTH 151
- GIVING BACK 159

THE END 168

INTRODUCTION

DEFINING WEALTH AND SUCCESS

What Does Wealth Mean to You?

Wealth means different things to different people. For some, it might be a certain amount of money in the bank or the ability to live a life of luxury without financial worries. For others, it could be the freedom to pursue passions, spend time with loved ones, or make a positive impact on the world. The first step in your journey to becoming wealthy fast is to understand what wealth means to you personally. This will help guide your decisions and keep you motivated.

The Difference Between Wealth and Income

It's crucial to distinguish between wealth and income. Income is the money you earn regularly, such as from a job or business. Wealth, on the other hand, is the total value of all your assets—your savings, investments, properties, and other valuable items—minus your debts. While a high income can help you build wealth, the key is to manage and grow your assets wisely. This guide will show you how to focus on building lasting wealth rather than just increasing your income.

Understanding Fast Wealth vs. Sustainable Wealth

Achieving wealth quickly often comes with higher risks and requires smart, strategic decisions. It's important to balance the desire for fast wealth with sustainable practices. Fast wealth can be achieved through high-return investments, entrepreneurial ventures, and leveraging opportunities, but it must be managed carefully to ensure it lasts. This guide will provide strategies for achieving wealth quickly while maintaining a long-term perspective.

CHAPTER ONE
SETTING THE FOUNDATION
Mindset And Attitude

To become wealthy quickly, you need to start with the right mindset and attitude. Your thoughts and beliefs shape your actions, and your actions determine your results. Let's explore how to cultivate a wealthy mindset, harness the power of positive thinking, and overcome limiting beliefs.

Cultivating a Wealthy Mindset

A wealthy mindset is about thinking and behaving in ways that attract and maintain wealth. Here are some key aspects:

1. Belief in Abundance: Believe that there is plenty of wealth to go around.

An abundance mindset sees opportunities rather than limitations. When you believe that wealth is attainable and that there are enough resources and opportunities for everyone, you're more likely to pursue and achieve financial success.

2. Taking Responsibility: Own your financial future. Instead of blaming external factors for financial setbacks, take responsibility for your financial decisions. This empowerment enables you to make proactive changes and take control of your wealth-building journey.

3. Focus on Growth: Always look for ways to improve and grow. Whether it's learning new skills, exploring new investment opportunities, or seeking out

new business ideas, a growth mindset is crucial. Continuous improvement and learning are key to building and maintaining wealth.

4. Long-Term Thinking: Think beyond immediate gains. Wealthy individuals often focus on long-term benefits rather than short-term rewards. They understand that building lasting wealth requires patience, planning, and consistent effort.

The Power of Positive Thinking

Positive thinking is a powerful tool that can significantly impact your journey to wealth. Here's how:

1. Optimism and Resilience: Positive thinking helps you stay optimistic and resilient in the face of challenges. When

you encounter obstacles or failures, a positive mindset enables you to view them as learning opportunities rather than insurmountable problems. This resilience is crucial for bouncing back and staying motivated.

2. Attracting Opportunities: A positive attitude can attract opportunities and people who can help you on your journey. Optimistic individuals are often seen as more approachable and trustworthy, which can open doors to new opportunities, collaborations, and partnerships.

3. Stress Reduction: Positive thinking reduces stress and improves mental well-being. When you're less stressed, you're better able to make clear, rational

financial decisions. Stress can cloud judgment and lead to poor financial choices, so maintaining a positive outlook is beneficial.

4. Enhanced Creativity: Positive thinkers are more likely to be creative and innovative. They see possibilities where others see problems. This creativity can lead to new business ideas, investment opportunities, and solutions to financial challenges.

Overcoming Limiting Beliefs

Limiting beliefs are negative thoughts and assumptions that hold you back from achieving your full potential. Here's how to identify and overcome them:

1. Identify Limiting Beliefs: The first step is to recognize the negative beliefs that are holding you back. Common limiting beliefs include thoughts like "I'll never be rich," "Money is the root of all evil," or "I'm not smart enough to invest." Write down these beliefs so you can address them.

2. Challenge Your Beliefs: Once you've identified your limiting beliefs, challenge their validity. Ask yourself if they are based on facts or simply negative assumptions. For example, if you believe you're not smart enough to invest, look for evidence that contradicts this belief. Many successful investors started with little knowledge and learned along the way.

3. Replace Negative Thoughts: Replace your limiting beliefs with positive, empowering ones. Instead of saying, "I'll never be rich," say, "I am capable of building wealth." Instead of thinking, "Money is the root of all evil," think, "Money is a tool that can be used for good." Positive affirmations can help reprogram your mind for success.

4. Surround Yourself with Positivity: Surround yourself with people who have a positive influence on you. Avoid naysayers and negative influences that reinforce limiting beliefs. Engage with mentors, peers, and resources that support your financial goals and encourage a positive mindset.

5. Take Action: Finally, take action to reinforce your new beliefs. Set small, achievable goals that move you toward wealth. Each success will build your confidence and reinforce your positive beliefs. As you see progress, your new mindset will become stronger.

SETTING CLEAR FINANCIAL GOALS

Setting clear financial goals is crucial for anyone looking to become wealthy quickly. Goals provide direction, motivation, and a way to measure progress. They help you stay focused and make informed decisions. In this section, we'll discuss the difference between short-term and long-term goals, how to set SMART goals for wealth creation, and the importance of having a financial plan.

Short-term vs. Long-term Goals

Short-term Goals: Short-term financial goals are objectives you aim to achieve within a relatively short period, typically within a year. These goals help you manage your immediate financial needs and lay the groundwork for longer-term ambitions. Examples of short-term goals include:

1. Saving a specific amount of money each month.

2. Paying off a small debt, such as a credit card balance.

3. Creating an emergency fund with three to six months' worth of living expenses.

4.   Learning a new skill that can increase your income.

Short-term goals are essential because they provide quick wins that boost your confidence and keep you motivated. They also help you build good financial habits, such as saving regularly and controlling spending.

Long-term Goals: Long-term financial goals take more time to achieve, typically several years or even decades. These goals are more ambitious and often involve larger amounts of money. Examples of long-term goals include:

1.   Saving for retirement.

2.   Buying a home or investment property.

3. Building a substantial investment portfolio.

4. Achieving financial independence.

Long-term goals require careful planning and a commitment to maintaining your financial discipline over time. They are crucial for creating lasting wealth and financial security.

SMART Goals for Wealth Creation

To set effective financial goals, it's helpful to use the SMART criteria. SMART stands for Specific, Measurable, Achievable, Relevant, and Time-bound. Here's how to apply it to wealth creation:

Specific: Your goals should be clear and specific. Instead of saying, "I want to save money," specify how much you want to save and for what purpose. For example, "I want to save $10,000 for a down payment on a house."

Measurable: Your goals should be measurable so you can track your progress. If your goal is to save $10,000, break it down into smaller milestones, such as saving $2,500 every three months. This way, you can measure your progress along the way.

Achievable: Set realistic goals that challenge you but are still attainable. If you set a goal that is too ambitious, you may become discouraged if you don't reach it. Consider your current financial situation and resources when setting goals. For example, if you're currently saving $200 a month, aiming to save

$500 a month might be a more achievable step up than jumping to $1,000.

Relevant: Your financial goals should align with your overall life goals and values. If becoming financially independent is important to you, make sure your financial goals contribute to that aim. For example, paying off high-interest debt is relevant because it frees up more money for investments and savings.

Time-bound: Set a deadline for your goals to create a sense of urgency and keep you focused. A deadline also helps you prioritize your actions. For example, "I want to save $10,000 in the next 12 months" gives you a clear time frame to work within.

The Importance of a Financial Plan

A financial plan is a comprehensive roadmap that outlines how you will achieve your financial goals. It includes your current financial situation, your goals, and the strategies you'll use to reach them. Here's why having a financial plan is important:

Clarity and Direction: A financial plan gives you a clear picture of where you are now and where you want to be. It helps you understand your financial strengths and weaknesses, so you can make informed decisions. With a plan, you know exactly what steps you need to take to achieve your goals.

Motivation and Focus: Having a plan keeps you motivated and focused. It's easy to get distracted or lose sight of your goals without a plan. A well-defined plan reminds you of your objectives and the reasons behind them, keeping you on track even when faced with challenges.

Better Decision-Making: A financial plan helps you make better financial decisions. It provides a framework for evaluating opportunities and risks. For example, if you're considering an investment, you can assess whether it aligns with your financial plan and helps you move closer to your goals.

Tracking Progress: A financial plan allows you to track your progress over time. By regularly reviewing your plan and comparing it to your actual financial situation, you can see if you're on track or need to adjust your strategies. This ongoing evaluation is crucial for staying aligned with your goals.

Financial Security: Finally, a financial plan provides financial security. It helps you prepare for unexpected expenses and emergencies by including provisions like an emergency fund. It also ensures that you're saving and investing enough to meet your long-term needs, such as retirement.

EDUCATION AND KNOWLEDGE

To achieve wealth quickly, education and knowledge are indispensable. They empower you to make informed financial decisions, recognize opportunities, and avoid costly mistakes. In this section, we'll cover the basics of financial literacy, the importance of investing in yourself, and the need for continuous learning and adaptation.

Financial Literacy Basics

Financial literacy is the ability to understand and manage your finances effectively. It involves knowing how to budget, save, invest, and handle debt. Here are the fundamental concepts you need to grasp:

1. Budgeting: Budgeting is the process of creating a plan for how you will spend and save your money. A budget helps you track your income and expenses, ensuring that you live within your means and set aside money for your goals. Start by listing your sources of income and all your expenses. Categorize your spending (e.g., housing, food, transportation, entertainment) and identify areas where you can cut back to save more.

2. Saving: Saving is crucial for building wealth. Aim to save a portion of your income regularly. A common recommendation is to save at least 20% of your income, but the exact amount can vary based on your financial goals.

Having an emergency fund (three to six months' worth of living expenses) is essential for financial security. Beyond that, save for specific goals such as buying a home, starting a business, or investing.

3. Investing: Investing involves using your money to purchase assets that have the potential to grow in value over time, such as stocks, bonds, real estate, or mutual funds. Investing can help your money grow faster than it would in a savings account, but it also carries risks. Understanding the basics of different investment options and how they work is key to making informed decisions.

4. Debt Management: Managing debt is an important aspect of financial

literacy. Not all debt is bad; for example, a mortgage or a student loan can be considered good debt if they help you build wealth or increase your earning potential. However, high-interest debt, such as credit card debt, can be detrimental. Learn strategies to pay off debt efficiently, such as the snowball or avalanche methods, and avoid taking on new debt unless it's necessary and manageable.

Investing in Yourself

Investing in yourself means dedicating time and resources to improve your skills, knowledge, and overall well-being. This type of investment often yields the highest returns. Here's how to invest in yourself:

1.   Education and Skills: Continuously improving your education and skills can significantly increase your earning potential. Consider taking courses, earning certifications, or obtaining a higher degree in your field. Skills that are in high demand, such as those in technology, finance, and healthcare, can lead to better job opportunities and higher salaries.

2.   Health and Well-being: Your physical and mental health are crucial to your ability to work and make sound financial decisions. Investing in a healthy lifestyle, including regular exercise, a balanced diet, and adequate rest, can improve your productivity and longevity. Don't hesitate to seek

professional help for mental health issues, as maintaining a positive mindset is key to financial success.

3. Networking: Building a strong professional network can open doors to new opportunities, mentorship, and valuable advice. Attend industry events, join professional organizations, and engage with peers and leaders in your field. Networking can lead to job offers, business partnerships, and investment opportunities.

4. Personal Development: Invest in your personal growth by reading books, attending seminars, and participating in workshops that focus on self-improvement and financial literacy. Personal development helps you build

the confidence and skills needed to pursue and achieve your financial goals.

Continuous Learning and Adaptation

The financial world is constantly evolving, and staying informed is crucial for long-term success. Here's why continuous learning and adaptation are important:

1. Keeping Up with Trends: Financial markets, investment strategies, and economic conditions change over time. Staying informed about the latest trends and developments helps you make timely and relevant financial decisions. Subscribe to financial news, follow market analysts, and participate in

online forums and discussions to stay updated.

2. Adapting to Change: Flexibility and adaptability are key traits for building and maintaining wealth. Whether it's a change in your career, a shift in the economy, or new investment opportunities, being able to adapt quickly can help you navigate challenges and capitalize on opportunities. Develop a mindset that embraces change and sees it as an opportunity for growth.

3. Learning from Mistakes: Everyone makes financial mistakes, but the important thing is to learn from them. Reflect on your financial decisions, identify what went wrong, and make adjustments to avoid similar mistakes in

the future. Continuous learning involves both acquiring new knowledge and improving from past experiences.

4. Expanding Your Horizons: Don't limit yourself to traditional forms of education. Explore diverse sources of knowledge, including podcasts, webinars, and online courses. Engaging with a variety of perspectives can provide new insights and innovative ideas for wealth creation.

CHAPTER TWO
INCOME GENERATION

Generating income is a critical aspect of becoming wealthy quickly. One effective way to do this is by focusing on high-income skills and careers. This section will discuss how to identify high-income skills, explore in-demand careers and professions, and examine the opportunities available in freelancing and consulting.

HIGH-INCOME SKILLS AND CAREERS

Identifying High-Income Skills

High-income skills are specialized abilities that are in high demand and can command significant pay. These skills often require a combination of education, training, and experience, but they provide a strong return on investment in terms of earning potential. Here are some steps to identify high-income skills:

1. Research Market Demand: Look at job market trends and reports to identify skills that are currently in high demand. Websites like LinkedIn, Glassdoor, and Indeed often publish insights into trending skills and job openings. Pay attention to industries experiencing growth, such as technology, healthcare, and finance.

2. Evaluate Your Interests and Strengths: Consider your personal interests and strengths when choosing a high-income skill to develop. It's easier

to excel in areas where you have a natural aptitude and genuine interest. For example, if you enjoy problem-solving and have a knack for numbers, skills in data analysis or financial planning might be a good fit.

3. Seek Advice from Professionals: Talk to professionals in various fields to gain insights into what skills are most valuable. Networking with industry experts can provide firsthand knowledge about the demand for certain skills and the potential income they can generate.

4. Consider Future Trends: Anticipate future trends and emerging fields. Technologies like artificial intelligence, machine learning, and blockchain are growing rapidly and creating new high-

income opportunities. Staying ahead of the curve can position you for lucrative roles in these innovative areas.

In-Demand Careers and Professions

Certain careers and professions are known for their high earning potential. Here are a few examples:

1. Technology:

A. Software Development: Software developers create applications and systems software. They are in high demand due to the increasing reliance on technology in all sectors.

B. Data Science: Data scientists analyze complex data to help organizations make informed decisions. This role requires strong analytical skills and knowledge of programming and statistics.

C. Cybersecurity: Cybersecurity professionals protect organizations from cyber threats. With the rise of digital data and cyberattacks, this field is critical and highly lucrative.

2. Healthcare:

A. Physicians and Surgeons: Medical professionals often earn high salaries due to the specialized education and training required.

B. Pharmacists: Pharmacists dispense medications and advise patients on their use, playing a crucial role in healthcare.

C. Nurse Practitioners: Advanced practice nurses who provide primary and specialty healthcare services.

3. Finance:

A. Investment Banking: Investment bankers help companies raise capital and provide financial advisory services. They often work long hours but are well-compensated.

B. Financial Planning: Financial planners assist individuals and businesses in managing their finances, including investments, taxes, and retirement planning.

C. Accountancy: Accountants manage financial records, ensuring accuracy and compliance with laws. Certified Public Accountants (CPAs) typically earn more.

4. Legal:

A. Lawyers: Lawyers advise and represent clients in legal matters.

Specializing in high-demand fields such as corporate law, intellectual property, or tax law can be especially profitable.

B. Compliance Officers: These professionals ensure that organizations comply with laws and regulations, particularly in highly regulated industries like finance and healthcare.

Freelancing and Consulting

Freelancing and consulting offer flexible opportunities to leverage high-income skills outside of traditional employment. Here's how you can capitalize on these paths:

1. Freelancing: Freelancers work independently, offering their skills and services to various clients. This path allows for flexibility and the potential to

earn a high income by taking on multiple projects. Popular freelancing fields include:

A. Graphic Design: Creating visual content for brands, marketing campaigns, and websites.

B. Writing and Content Creation: Producing articles, blog posts, and marketing copy.

C. Web Development: Building and maintaining websites for clients.

2. Consulting: Consultants provide expert advice to organizations to help them solve problems and improve performance. This can be done on a contract basis or through a consulting firm. Key areas for consulting include:

A. Business Consulting: Advising companies on strategy, operations, and management.

B. IT Consulting: Helping organizations implement and manage technology solutions.

C. Financial Consulting: Offering guidance on financial planning, investments, and risk management.

Benefits of Freelancing and Consulting:

1. Flexibility: Freelancers and consultants can choose their clients and projects, giving them control over their schedules and work-life balance.

2. Higher Earnings Potential: By setting their rates and taking on multiple clients, freelancers and

consultants can potentially earn more than in traditional roles.

3. Skill Development: Working with diverse clients and projects helps freelancers and consultants continuously develop and refine their skills.

How to Succeed in Freelancing and Consulting:

1. Build a Strong Portfolio: Showcase your skills and experience with a professional portfolio. Include examples of past work, testimonials, and case studies.

2. Network and Market Yourself: Use professional networks like LinkedIn to connect with potential clients. Attend

industry events and engage in online communities to increase your visibility.

3. Deliver Quality Work: Consistently provide high-quality work to build a strong reputation. Satisfied clients are likely to provide repeat business and referrals.

ENTREPRENEURSHIP

Entrepreneurship is a powerful way to generate wealth quickly. It involves starting and managing a business with the aim of making a profit. This section will explore how to start a business, find profitable niches, and scale your business quickly.

Starting a Business

Starting a business is an exciting but challenging endeavor. It requires careful planning, dedication, and a willingness to take risks. Here's a step-by-step guide to getting started:

1. Idea Generation: Begin by brainstorming business ideas. Think about your interests, skills, and market needs. Look for problems that need solving or gaps in the market that you can fill. Your business idea should be something you're passionate about and that has the potential to generate profit.

2. Market Research: Conduct thorough market research to validate your business idea. Identify your target audience, understand their needs and preferences, and analyze your competition. Market research helps you determine if there is a demand for your

product or service and how you can differentiate yourself from competitors.

3. Business Plan: Develop a detailed business plan outlining your business goals, target market, marketing strategies, operational plan, and financial projections. A business plan serves as a roadmap for your business and is essential for securing funding from investors or lenders.

4. Funding: Determine how much capital you need to start your business and explore funding options. These may include personal savings, loans, grants, or investments from venture capitalists or angel investors. Ensure you have enough funds to cover initial expenses

and sustain your business until it becomes profitable.

5. Legal Structure: Choose the legal structure of your business, such as a sole proprietorship, partnership, limited liability company (LLC), or corporation. Each structure has different legal and tax implications. Register your business and obtain any necessary licenses and permits.

6. Setting Up Operations: Set up your business operations, including finding a location (if needed), purchasing equipment and supplies, and setting up your website and online presence. Hire employees if necessary and establish your operational processes.

7. Launching: Plan a launch strategy to introduce your business to the market. This could include a grand opening event, promotional offers, or a marketing campaign. Use social media, email marketing, and other channels to reach your target audience and generate buzz about your business.

Finding Profitable Niches

A niche market is a specific segment of a larger market that has unique needs and preferences. Finding a profitable niche can help you stand out from competitors and attract a loyal customer base. Here's how to identify and capitalize on a profitable niche:

1. Identify Your Interests and Strengths: Consider your own interests,

skills, and expertise. Starting a business in a field you're passionate about and knowledgeable in increases your chances of success.

2. Analyze Market Trends: Look for emerging trends and shifts in consumer behavior. Use tools like Google Trends, social media, and industry reports to identify potential niche markets that are growing in popularity.

3. Evaluate Competition: Assess the level of competition in your potential niche. A profitable niche should have demand but not be overly saturated. Look for gaps or underserved areas where you can offer something unique.

4. Understand Customer Pain Points: Identify the specific problems or pain

points that your target customers face. Develop products or services that address these issues effectively. Conduct surveys, interviews, and focus groups to gather insights directly from your target audience.

5. Test Your Idea: Before fully committing, test your niche idea with a minimum viable product (MVP) or a pilot launch. Gather feedback and measure demand to validate your concept. Adjust your offerings based on the feedback you receive.

Scaling Your Business Quickly

Scaling a business involves expanding your operations to increase revenue and market share without compromising quality. Here are strategies to scale your business quickly:

1. Standardize Processes: Develop standardized processes for your operations to ensure consistency and efficiency. Document your workflows and create training materials to streamline onboarding for new employees.

2. Leverage Technology: Use technology to automate and optimize various aspects of your business, such as inventory management, customer relationship management (CRM), and marketing automation. This reduces manual effort and allows you to handle increased demand.

3. Expand Your Market Reach: Identify new markets or customer segments to target. Consider expanding geographically, launching new products or services, or entering related industries. Diversifying your offerings can increase your revenue streams.

4. Build a Strong Team: Hire skilled and experienced employees who can support your growth. Focus on building a strong leadership team and delegate responsibilities to ensure effective management as you scale.

5. Secure Funding: To scale quickly, you may need additional capital. Explore funding options such as venture capital, private equity, or business loans.

Prepare a compelling growth plan to attract investors.

6. Optimize Marketing Efforts: Invest in marketing strategies that can scale with your business, such as digital marketing, social media advertising, and influencer partnerships. Use data analytics to measure the effectiveness of your marketing campaigns and adjust your strategies accordingly.

7. Focus on Customer Retention: While acquiring new customers is important, retaining existing customers is crucial for long-term success. Provide exceptional customer service, create loyalty programs, and continuously improve your offerings based on customer feedback.

8. Strategic Partnerships: Form strategic partnerships with other businesses to expand your reach and capabilities. Collaborations can provide access to new markets, resources, and expertise that can accelerate your growth.

SIDE HUSTLES AND GIG ECONOMY

Engaging in side hustles and participating in the gig economy can be an effective strategy for generating additional income. This approach allows you to diversify your income streams, maximize your earnings, and increase your financial security. In this section, we'll explore popular and lucrative side hustles, provide tips for maximizing your earnings, and discuss how to balance multiple income streams effectively.

Popular and Lucrative Side Hustles

A side hustle is any type of employment undertaken in addition to one's full-time job. It provides supplemental income and can be an avenue to pursue passions or interests. Here are some popular and lucrative side hustles:

1. Freelance Writing: If you have strong writing skills, freelance writing can be a highly profitable side hustle. You can write articles, blog posts, or copy for businesses. Platforms like Upwork, Fiverr, and Freelancer can help you find clients.

2. Graphic Design: Graphic designers can create logos, social media graphics, and marketing materials for clients. This side hustle requires creativity and proficiency in design software like Adobe Photoshop or Illustrator.

3. Tutoring: Offering tutoring services in subjects you excel in can be both rewarding and lucrative. You can tutor students in academic subjects, standardized test preparation, or even teach languages. Websites like Wyzant and Tutor.com can help you find students.

4. Ridesharing and Delivery Services: Driving for companies like Uber, Lyft, DoorDash, or Postmates can be a flexible side hustle. It allows you to work

on your schedule and earn money based on the number of rides or deliveries you complete.

5. E-commerce: Selling products online through platforms like Etsy, eBay, or Amazon can generate significant income. You can sell handmade crafts, vintage items, or dropship products directly from suppliers to customers.

6. Photography: If you have a passion for photography, consider offering your services for events, portraits, or stock photos. Websites like Shutterstock and Adobe Stock allow you to sell your photos to a broader audience.

7. Pet Sitting and Dog Walking: For animal lovers, pet sitting and dog

walking can be enjoyable and profitable. Websites like Rover and Wag! connect pet owners with reliable pet sitters and dog walkers.

8. Fitness Training: If you're a certified fitness trainer or have expertise in a specific type of exercise, offering personal training sessions or group classes can be a high-earning side hustle.

Maximizing Your Earnings

To make the most of your side hustle, it's important to employ strategies that maximize your earnings. Here are some tips:

1. Choose High-Demand Niches: Focus on side hustles that are in high demand. Research the market to identify

trends and gaps where your skills can provide value. High-demand niches often command higher rates.

2. Set Competitive Rates: Research what others in your field are charging and set your rates accordingly. Don't undervalue your services; ensure your rates reflect the quality and expertise you bring. Consider offering package deals or discounts for repeat clients to encourage long-term engagements.

3. Improve Your Skills: Continuously improve your skills through training, certifications, and practice. The more skilled and knowledgeable you are, the more you can charge for your services. Invest in courses, attend workshops, and stay updated with industry trends.

4. Market Yourself Effectively: Promote your side hustle through various channels. Use social media, create a professional website, and network with potential clients. Positive reviews and word-of-mouth referrals can also significantly boost your client base.

5. Optimize Your Time: Manage your time efficiently to balance your side hustle with your full-time job. Use productivity tools to schedule tasks, set deadlines, and track your progress. Prioritize high-paying tasks and minimize time spent on low-value activities.

6. Leverage Technology: Use technology to streamline your side

hustle operations. For instance, use accounting software to manage your finances, scheduling tools to organize your tasks, and marketing platforms to reach a wider audience.

Balancing Multiple Income Streams

Balancing multiple income streams requires careful planning and organization. Here's how to manage them effectively:

1. Create a Schedule: Develop a weekly or monthly schedule that allocates time for your full-time job, side hustles, and personal life. Ensure you dedicate enough time to each income stream without overloading yourself.

2. Set Clear Goals: Establish clear financial and personal goals for each of your income streams. Having specific targets helps you stay focused and motivated. Regularly review and adjust your goals as needed.

3. Prioritize Tasks: Prioritize your tasks based on urgency and importance. Focus on high-impact activities that generate the most income or are crucial for your long-term success. Delegate or outsource low-priority tasks if possible.

4. Maintain Work-Life Balance: Balancing multiple income streams shouldn't come at the expense of your health and well-being. Make sure to schedule downtime and activities that help you relax and recharge. Avoid

burnout by setting boundaries and taking regular breaks.

5. Track Your Finances: Keep detailed records of your income and expenses for each side hustle. Use budgeting and financial tracking tools to monitor your cash flow and ensure you're meeting your financial goals. This also helps during tax season when you need to report multiple sources of income.

6. Stay Flexible: Be adaptable and open to adjusting your strategies as needed. If one income stream isn't performing as expected, reassess and explore new opportunities. Flexibility allows you to pivot and make the most of changing market conditions.

CHAPTER THREE
SMART INVESTING

Smart investing is a cornerstone of building wealth quickly. Among the various investment opportunities, the stock market stands out as one of the most accessible and potentially lucrative. This section will cover the basics of stock market investing, the potential of high-growth stocks, and how to leverage stock options effectively.

STOCK MARKET INVESTMENTS
Basics of Stock Market Investing

Investing in the stock market involves buying shares of publicly traded companies. When you purchase a share, you own a small part of that company and have the potential to earn money through dividends and capital gains. Here's a breakdown of the key concepts you need to understand:

1. Stocks and Shares: Stocks represent ownership in a company. When you buy a share, you become a shareholder and own a fraction of that company. The value of your shares can increase or decrease based on the company's performance and market conditions.

2. Stock Exchanges: Stocks are bought and sold on stock exchanges, such as the New York Stock Exchange (NYSE) or the Nasdaq. These exchanges provide a platform for investors to trade shares in a regulated environment.

3. Market Indexes: Market indexes, like the S&P 500 or the Dow Jones Industrial Average, track the performance of a group of stocks. These indexes give you an idea of how the overall market or specific sectors are performing.

4. Dividends: Dividends are payments made by a company to its shareholders from its profits. Not all companies pay dividends, but those that do provide a regular income stream in addition to potential capital gains.

5. Capital Gains: Capital gains occur when you sell a stock for more than you paid for it. The difference between the purchase price and the selling price is your profit.

6. Risk and Return: Investing in the stock market involves risk, as the value of stocks can fluctuate. However, higher risk can also lead to higher returns. Diversifying your investments across different sectors and companies can help manage risk.

High-Growth Stocks

High-growth stocks are shares in companies that are expected to grow at an above-average rate compared to other companies in the market. Investing in high-growth stocks can lead to significant returns, but they also come with higher risk. Here's how to identify and invest in high-growth stocks:

1. Identifying High-Growth Stocks: Look for companies with strong revenue

growth, innovative products or services, and a competitive edge in their industry. High-growth companies often reinvest their profits into expansion, which can lead to rapid growth.

2. Key Indicators:

A. Revenue Growth: Consistent and strong revenue growth is a sign that a company is expanding and increasing its market share.

B. Earnings Per Share (EPS): A rising EPS indicates that the company is becoming more profitable.

C. Price-to-Earnings (P/E) Ratio: A high P/E ratio can indicate that investors expect high growth in the future. However, it's important to compare this ratio to industry peers.

3. Industries with High-Growth Potential: Some industries are more likely to contain high-growth companies. These include technology, healthcare, renewable energy, and e-commerce. Companies in these sectors often innovate and expand rapidly.

4. Examples of High-Growth Stocks:

A. Technology: Companies like Apple, Amazon, and Tesla have shown significant growth due to their innovative products and services.

B. Healthcare: Biotechnology and pharmaceutical companies that develop new treatments and medications often experience high growth.

C. Renewable Energy: Companies focusing on renewable energy sources like solar, wind, and electric vehicles are poised for growth as the world shifts towards sustainability.

Leveraging Stock Options

Stock options are financial instruments that give you the right, but not the obligation, to buy or sell a stock at a predetermined price within a specific period. They can be used to hedge risk, generate income, or speculate on stock price movements. Here's how to leverage stock options effectively:

1. Types of Stock Options:

A. Call Options: Give you the right to buy a stock at a specific price. Investors use call options when they expect the stock price to rise.

B. Put Options: Give you the right to sell a stock at a specific price. Investors use put options when they expect the stock price to fall.

2. Basic Strategies:

A. Buying Calls: Purchase call options if you believe a stock's price will rise. This strategy allows you to control a larger number of shares with less capital than buying the stock outright.

B. Buying Puts: Purchase put options if you believe a stock's price will fall. This strategy can protect your portfolio against declines in the stock market.

C. Selling Covered Calls: If you own shares of a stock, you can sell call options against those shares. This generates income from the option premiums while you continue to hold the stock.

3. Benefits of Stock Options:

A. Leverage: Options allow you to control more shares with less money, increasing potential returns.

B. Risk Management: Options can hedge against potential losses in your portfolio.

C. Income Generation: Selling options, such as covered calls, can generate additional income.

4. Risks of Stock Options:

A. Complexity: Options are more complex than buying and selling stocks. It's important to understand how they work before investing.

B. Expiration Dates: Options have expiration dates, after which they become worthless if not exercised.

C. Potential Losses: While options can amplify gains, they can also amplify losses. You can lose the entire premium paid for the option.

REAL ESTATE INVESTING

Real estate investing is a popular strategy for building wealth and generating passive income. It involves purchasing properties with the intention of earning a return on investment through rental income, appreciation, or both. In this section, we'll explore different real estate investment strategies, including flipping properties and investing in rental properties for passive income.

Real Estate Investment Strategies

Real estate offers a variety of investment strategies, each with its own benefits and risks. Here are some common strategies:

1. Buy and Hold: This strategy involves purchasing properties with the intention of holding onto them for the long term. Investors aim to generate passive income through rental payments while benefiting from property appreciation over time. Buy-and-hold investors typically look for properties in stable markets with strong rental demand.

2. Fix and Flip: Fix and flip investors purchase distressed properties, renovate them to increase their value, and then sell them for a profit. This strategy requires careful market analysis, property valuation, and renovation planning. Successful fix and flip investors often have experience in construction, real estate, or home remodeling.

3. Wholesaling: Wholesaling involves finding discounted properties and assigning the purchase contract to another investor for a fee. Wholesalers act as intermediaries between sellers and buyers and typically don't take ownership of the property. This strategy

requires strong negotiation skills and a network of investors.

4. Real Estate Investment Trusts (REITs): REITs are companies that own, operate, or finance income-producing real estate. Investors can buy shares of REITs on the stock market, providing exposure to real estate without directly owning properties. REITs typically pay dividends to shareholders, making them a popular choice for passive income investors.

5. Real Estate Crowdfunding: Real estate crowdfunding platforms allow individual investors to pool their money to invest in properties or real estate projects. These platforms offer opportunities to invest in commercial or

residential properties with lower capital requirements compared to traditional real estate investing. Investors can choose from a variety of projects based on their investment goals and risk tolerance.

Flipping Properties

Flipping properties involves purchasing homes at a discounted price, renovating them to increase their value, and then selling them for a profit. Here's how the process typically works:

1. Property Acquisition: Flippers search for distressed properties, such as foreclosures, short sales, or homes in need of significant repairs. They often look for properties with potential for value appreciation after renovations.

2. Renovation and Improvement: After purchasing a property, flippers invest in renovations and upgrades to improve its appeal and market value. This may include cosmetic improvements like painting and flooring, as well as structural repairs like plumbing or electrical work.

3. Market Analysis: Flippers analyze the local real estate market to determine the optimal selling price for the renovated property. They consider factors such as comparable sales (comps), neighborhood trends, and buyer preferences.

4. Selling the Property: Once renovations are complete, flippers list the property for sale on the market.

They may work with real estate agents to market the property effectively and attract potential buyers. The goal is to sell the property quickly and at a profit.

5. Calculating Profit: Flippers calculate their profit by subtracting the purchase price, renovation costs, and selling expenses from the final sale price. Successful flips result in a positive return on investment (ROI) that reflects the effort and capital invested in the project.

Rental Properties for Passive Income

Investing in rental properties involves purchasing homes or apartment buildings and renting them out to tenants. Here's how rental property investing works:

1. Property Acquisition: Investors identify properties in desirable locations with strong rental demand. They consider factors such as proximity to amenities, job opportunities, and schools when selecting properties.

2. Financing the Purchase: Investors may use financing options like mortgages or private loans to purchase rental properties. They typically aim for a favorable loan-to-value (LTV) ratio and secure financing with competitive interest rates.

3. Tenant Screening and Management: Once the property is acquired, investors screen potential

tenants to find reliable renters who can pay rent on time and maintain the property. Property management tasks may include rent collection, maintenance, and addressing tenant concerns.

4. Generating Rental Income: Rental property investors earn income from monthly rent payments collected from tenants. The rental income should cover expenses such as mortgage payments, property taxes, insurance, maintenance, and vacancies.

5. Property Appreciation: Over time, rental properties may appreciate in value due to factors such as inflation, market demand, and property improvements. Investors can benefit

from equity growth and potential capital gains when selling the property in the future.

6. Tax Benefits: Rental property investors may qualify for various tax deductions and incentives, including depreciation, mortgage interest deductions, and property tax deductions. These tax benefits can help offset rental income and reduce tax liabilities.

CRYPTOCURRENCY AND DIGITAL ASSETS

Cryptocurrency and digital assets have emerged as a revolutionary force in the financial world, offering decentralized and borderless alternatives to traditional currencies and assets. In this section, we will delve into the basics of cryptocurrencies, explore high-potential digital assets, and discuss the associated risks and rewards.

Introduction to Cryptocurrencies

Cryptocurrencies are digital or virtual currencies that use cryptography for security and operate on decentralized networks based on blockchain technology. Unlike traditional currencies issued by governments, cryptocurrencies are not controlled by any central authority, such as a central bank. Here are some key characteristics of cryptocurrencies:

1. Decentralization: Cryptocurrencies operate on decentralized networks of computers, known as blockchain

networks. These networks are distributed across multiple nodes, making them resistant to censorship and tampering.

2. Blockchain Technology: Blockchain is a distributed ledger technology that records all transactions across a network of computers. Each transaction is verified by network participants and added to a block, which is then linked to previous blocks, creating a chain of blocks (hence the name blockchain).

3. Security and Transparency: Cryptocurrencies use cryptographic techniques to secure transactions and control the creation of new units. Transactions are transparent and

publicly recorded on the blockchain, allowing anyone to verify them.

4. Limited Supply: Many cryptocurrencies have a fixed supply or a predetermined issuance schedule, which can create scarcity and potentially increase their value over time. For example, Bitcoin has a maximum supply of 21 million coins.

5. Digital Wallets: To store and manage cryptocurrencies, users use digital wallets, which can be software-based or hardware-based. Digital wallets provide secure access to the user's cryptocurrency holdings and facilitate transactions.

Some of the most well-known cryptocurrencies include Bitcoin (BTC),

Ethereum (ETH), Ripple (XRP), Litecoin (LTC), and Bitcoin Cash (BCH). Each cryptocurrency has its own unique features, use cases, and community of supporters.

High-Potential Digital Assets

While Bitcoin remains the most prominent and widely adopted cryptocurrency, the digital asset space is constantly evolving, with new projects and innovations emerging regularly. Here are some high-potential digital assets to watch:

1. Ethereum (ETH): Ethereum is a decentralized platform that enables the creation of smart contracts and decentralized applications (DApps). It has a large and active developer

community, making it a hub for innovation in the blockchain space.

2. Decentralized Finance (DeFi) Tokens: DeFi tokens are cryptocurrencies that facilitate decentralized financial services, such as lending, borrowing, and trading, without the need for traditional intermediaries like banks. Examples include Aave (AAVE), Uniswap (UNI), and Compound (COMP).

3. Non-Fungible Tokens (NFTs): NFTs are unique digital assets that represent ownership or proof of authenticity of digital or physical items. They have gained popularity in digital art, collectibles, gaming, and entertainment industries. Platforms like

Ethereum-based OpenSea and Binance Smart Chain-based BakerySwap facilitate NFT trading.

4. Layer-1 Blockchain Platforms: Layer-1 blockchain platforms are protocols that enable the development and deployment of decentralized applications. Examples include Polkadot (DOT), Cardano (ADA), and Solana (SOL), which offer scalability, interoperability, and other advanced features.

5. Privacy Coins: Privacy coins focus on enhancing user privacy and anonymity in transactions. Examples include Monero (XMR), Zcash (ZEC), and Dash (DASH), which use advanced

cryptographic techniques to obfuscate transaction details.

Risks and Rewards

Investing in cryptocurrencies and digital assets offers the potential for significant returns but also comes with inherent risks. Here are some of the main risks and rewards associated with cryptocurrency investments:

Risks:

1. Volatility: Cryptocurrency markets are highly volatile, with prices subject to rapid and unpredictable fluctuations. This volatility can lead to significant gains but also substantial losses.

2. Regulatory Uncertainty: The regulatory landscape for cryptocurrencies is still evolving, with

governments around the world taking varying approaches to regulation. Regulatory changes or crackdowns can impact the value and legality of cryptocurrencies.

3. Security Concerns: Cryptocurrency exchanges and wallets are susceptible to hacking and cybersecurity threats. Investors risk losing their funds if they store their cryptocurrencies on insecure platforms or fall victim to phishing attacks.

4. Lack of Consumer Protections: Unlike traditional financial systems, cryptocurrencies offer limited consumer protections and recourse in case of fraud, theft, or disputes. Investors must

exercise caution and perform due diligence before investing.

Rewards:

1. Potential for High Returns: Cryptocurrencies have delivered exceptional returns for early adopters and investors who timed their investments well. Some cryptocurrencies have experienced exponential growth, creating millionaires and even billionaires.

2. Decentralization and Financial Freedom: Cryptocurrencies promote financial sovereignty and empower individuals to control their own assets without relying on intermediaries. They offer access to financial services for

unbanked populations and enable censorship-resistant transactions.

3. Innovation and Disruption: Cryptocurrencies and blockchain technology have the potential to revolutionize various industries, including finance, supply chain, healthcare, and gaming. They enable new business models, improve efficiency, and foster global collaboration.

4. Diversification and Portfolio Hedge: Cryptocurrencies provide diversification benefits and can serve as a hedge against traditional assets like stocks and bonds. They have low correlation with traditional markets,

offering potential portfolio protection during times of economic uncertainty.

ALTERNATIVE INVESTMENTS

Alternative investments offer investors opportunities beyond traditional asset classes like stocks, bonds, and cash. These investments often have unique characteristics and can provide diversification benefits to a portfolio. In this section, we will explore three popular alternative investment options: peer-to-peer lending, commodities and precious metals, and art and collectibles.

Peer-to-Peer Lending

Peer-to-peer (P2P) lending platforms connect borrowers with investors willing to lend money for a return. This form of lending bypasses traditional financial institutions, allowing individuals to access financing outside of banks. Here's how peer-to-peer lending works:

1. Platform Selection: Investors choose a P2P lending platform that matches their investment criteria and risk tolerance. These platforms vary in terms of borrower screening, loan types, and interest rates offered.

2. Borrower Evaluation: P2P lending platforms assess borrowers' creditworthiness through credit checks, income verification, and other risk assessment criteria. Investors can review borrowers' profiles and loan details before deciding to invest.

3. Investment Allocation: Investors can diversify their investments across

multiple loans to spread risk. They can choose the amount to invest in each loan based on factors such as borrower credit rating, loan purpose, and interest rate.

4. Interest Income: Investors earn interest income from the loans they fund. The interest rates vary depending on the borrower's creditworthiness and the terms of the loan. Some platforms offer fixed-rate loans, while others use variable rates.

5. Loan Repayment: Borrowers make regular payments on their loans, which include principal and interest. Investors receive a portion of these payments based on their investment in the loan. The loan term and repayment schedule are predetermined.

6. Risk Management: P2P lending carries risks, including borrower default, platform insolvency, and liquidity constraints. Investors should conduct thorough due diligence, diversify their investments, and monitor their portfolios regularly to manage risk.

Commodities and Precious Metals

Commodities are raw materials or primary agricultural products that can be bought and sold, such as oil, gold, silver, corn, and coffee. Investing in commodities and precious metals can offer diversification benefits and a hedge against inflation. Here's how investors can access these markets:

1. Physical Ownership: Investors can purchase physical commodities like gold

bars, silver coins, or barrels of oil for direct ownership. Physical ownership provides tangible assets that can be stored securely or held as part of a precious metals IRA.

2. Futures Contracts: Futures contracts allow investors to buy or sell commodities at a predetermined price on a future date. Futures trading requires specialized knowledge and carries the risk of leverage and price volatility.

3. Exchange-Traded Funds (ETFs): ETFs offer a convenient way to invest in commodities and precious metals without the complexities of futures trading. Commodity ETFs track the price movements of underlying

commodities or commodity indexes and can be bought and sold on stock exchanges.

4. Mutual Funds: Mutual funds focused on commodities and natural resources invest in companies involved in commodity production, extraction, or distribution. These funds provide exposure to commodity-related industries, such as energy, mining, and agriculture.

5. Storage and Security: Investing in physical commodities requires consideration of storage and security arrangements. Precious metals, in particular, should be stored in secure facilities to protect against theft and damage.

Art and Collectibles

Art and collectibles encompass a wide range of tangible assets, including paintings, sculptures, rare coins, vintage cars, and antiques. Investing in art and collectibles can offer potential appreciation and aesthetic enjoyment. Here's what investors should know:

1. Market Research: Art and collectibles markets are specialized and subjective, requiring research and expertise to navigate. Investors should study market trends, auction results, and the reputation of artists or brands before making purchases.

2. Authentication and Valuation: Authenticity and provenance are critical factors in the value of art and

collectibles. Investors should obtain certificates of authenticity and seek expert appraisals to verify the legitimacy and quality of their acquisitions.

3. Diversification: Like other alternative investments, art and collectibles can provide diversification benefits to a portfolio. Investors should consider diversifying across different asset classes, genres, artists, or periods to mitigate risk.

4. Liquidity and Storage: Art and collectibles are illiquid assets that may take time to sell and realize returns. Investors should be prepared for extended holding periods and consider storage and insurance costs for their collections.

5. Emerging Markets: Emerging markets, such as contemporary art, street art, and cultural artifacts, offer opportunities for growth and discovery. Investors can explore emerging artists and niche categories for potential appreciation and investment returns.

CHAPTER FOUR
FINANCIAL MANAGEMENT

Financial management is the cornerstone of achieving financial stability and building wealth. In this chapter, we will delve into essential practices of budgeting and saving, which are fundamental to effective financial management.

BUDGETING AND SAVING

Budgeting and saving are like the blueprint and foundation of a solid financial plan. They provide structure and discipline to your finances, helping you make the most of your income and achieve your financial goals.

Creating and Sticking to a Budget

1. Assess Your Finances: Begin by understanding your financial situation. Calculate your income, including salaries, wages, bonuses, and any other sources of income. Then, list all your expenses, including fixed expenses like rent or mortgage payments, utilities, groceries, transportation, and discretionary spending like entertainment and dining out.

2. Set Financial Goals: Determine what you want to achieve financially. Whether it's saving for a down payment on a house, paying off debt, building an emergency fund, or investing for retirement, having clear goals will guide

your budgeting efforts and keep you motivated.

3. Track Your Spending: Keep a record of all your expenses for at least a month. This will help you understand where your money is going and identify areas where you can cut back or optimize spending.

4. Allocate Your Income: Once you have a clear picture of your income and expenses, allocate your income to different categories based on priority. Start with necessities like housing, utilities, groceries, and debt payments, then allocate funds to savings, investments, and discretionary spending.

5. Adjust as Needed: Your financial situation and priorities may change over time, so it's essential to review and adjust your budget regularly. Be flexible and willing to make changes as necessary to stay on track with your financial goals.

Cutting Unnecessary Expenses

1. Identify Non-Essential Expenses: Review your expenses to identify discretionary spending that can be reduced or eliminated. This may include dining out frequently, subscription services you don't use, impulse purchases, or luxury items.

2. Prioritize Needs Over Wants: Distinguish between needs and wants. Focus on covering your essential needs

first before allocating funds to non-essential items. Ask yourself if a purchase is necessary or if it aligns with your financial goals before making it.

3. Practice Frugality: Look for ways to save money without sacrificing quality of life. This could mean shopping for discounts, buying generic brands, using coupons, or negotiating better deals on services like cable or internet.

4. Limit Impulse Purchases: Avoid making impulse purchases by implementing a waiting period before buying non-essential items. Take time to consider whether you truly need or want the item before making a purchase.

5. Find Creative Alternatives: Seek out low-cost or free alternatives to

expensive activities or purchases. For example, instead of going to the movies, have a movie night at home. Instead of dining out, try cooking at home or hosting potluck dinners with friends.

Saving Strategies for Rapid Wealth Accumulation

1. Automate Your Savings: Set up automatic transfers from your checking account to your savings or investment accounts. This ensures that you consistently save a portion of your income without having to think about it.

2. Pay Yourself First: Treat savings as a non-negotiable expense and prioritize it before spending on discretionary items. Aim to save a percentage of your

income, such as 10-20%, before allocating funds to other expenses.

3. Emergency Fund: Build an emergency fund to cover unexpected expenses or financial emergencies. Aim to save at least three to six months' worth of living expenses in a separate, easily accessible account.

4. Invest for Growth: Consider investing your savings in assets that have the potential for long-term growth, such as stocks, bonds, mutual funds, or real estate. Diversify your investments to minimize risk and maximize returns.

5. Reduce Debt: Prioritize paying off high-interest debt, such as credit card balances or personal loans. Use strategies like the debt snowball or debt

avalanche method to accelerate debt repayment and free up more money for savings and investments.

DEBT MANAGEMENT

Debt management is a crucial aspect of personal finance that involves effectively managing your debt to achieve financial stability and freedom. In this section, we'll explore the concept of good debt versus bad debt, strategies for rapid debt repayment, and leveraging debt for wealth creation.

Good Debt vs. Bad Debt

Understanding the difference between good debt and bad debt is essential for making informed financial decisions.

Good Debt:

Good debt is debt that helps you build wealth or improve your financial situation in the long run. It typically involves borrowing money to invest in assets that have the potential to increase in value or generate income. Examples of good debt include:

1. Mortgages: Taking out a mortgage to purchase a home can be considered good debt because it allows you to acquire an asset (real estate) that may appreciate in value over time. Additionally, mortgage interest payments may be tax-deductible in some cases.

2. Student Loans: Borrowing money to invest in education can be seen as an

investment in your future earning potential. While student loans can be a significant financial burden, a college degree or vocational training can lead to higher-paying job opportunities in the future.

3. Business Loans: Borrowing money to start or expand a business can be considered good debt if it leads to increased revenue and profitability. Business loans may be used to finance equipment purchases, inventory, marketing campaigns, or expansion projects.

Bad Debt:

Bad debt is debt that does not contribute to your long-term financial well-being and may hinder your financial progress.

It typically involves borrowing money for consumption or depreciating assets. Examples of bad debt include:

1. Credit Card Debt: Using credit cards to finance discretionary purchases, such as luxury items, vacations, or dining out, can lead to high-interest debt that accumulates quickly and becomes difficult to repay.

2. High-Interest Consumer Loans: Taking out payday loans, auto title loans, or high-interest personal loans to cover everyday expenses or emergencies can trap borrowers in a cycle of debt due to exorbitant interest rates and fees.

3. Car Loans: While car loans may be necessary for purchasing a vehicle, financing a car with high-interest rates

or long repayment terms can result in negative equity and financial strain.

Strategies for Rapid Debt Repayment

If you have accumulated debt, adopting strategies for rapid debt repayment can help you regain control of your finances and become debt-free sooner.

1. Debt Snowball Method: The debt snowball method involves paying off your debts in order from smallest to largest balance while making minimum payments on all other debts. Once the smallest debt is paid off, you roll the amount you were paying on that debt into the next smallest debt, and so on. This method provides psychological

motivation by offering quick wins and momentum.

2. Debt Avalanche Method: The debt avalanche method prioritizes paying off debts with the highest interest rates first while making minimum payments on all other debts. By focusing on high-interest debt, you can save money on interest charges and pay off your debts more efficiently over time.

3. Increase Income and Decrease Expenses: Boosting your income through side hustles, freelancing, or a second job can provide additional funds to put towards debt repayment. Additionally, cutting expenses and reallocating discretionary spending

towards debt repayment can accelerate your progress.

4. Negotiate Lower Interest Rates: Contact your creditors to negotiate lower interest rates or explore debt consolidation options to streamline your debt payments and reduce overall interest costs.

5. Stay Focused and Motivated: Debt repayment requires discipline and perseverance. Stay focused on your goal of becoming debt-free and celebrate milestones along the way to keep yourself motivated.

Leveraging Debt for Wealth Creation

While debt can be a double-edged sword, used wisely, it can be a powerful tool for wealth creation.

1. Real Estate Investing: Borrowing money to invest in real estate properties can provide opportunities for rental income, property appreciation, and portfolio diversification. Leveraging real estate debt allows investors to amplify their returns through leverage.

2. Business Expansion: Taking out loans to expand or scale a business can fuel growth and increase profitability. Whether it's investing in new equipment, hiring additional staff, or expanding into new markets, strategic

debt financing can help businesses capitalize on opportunities for expansion.

3. Investing in Stocks and Bonds: Margin borrowing allows investors to borrow money from brokerage firms to purchase stocks and bonds. While margin trading carries risks, it can amplify returns in a rising market environment when used judiciously.

4. Education and Skills Development: Investing in education or acquiring new skills through training programs or certifications can enhance earning potential and career opportunities. Student loans or personal loans used for education may be considered an

investment in yourself and your future earning capacity.

TAX OPTIMIZATION

Tax optimization is a crucial aspect of financial planning that involves strategically managing your finances to minimize tax liabilities and maximize after-tax returns. In this section, we'll explore the fundamentals of tax optimization, including understanding taxes and wealth, utilizing tax-advantaged accounts, and implementing legal strategies to minimize tax liabilities.

Understanding Taxes and Wealth

Taxes play a significant role in wealth accumulation and preservation. Understanding how taxes impact your finances is essential for making informed decisions and optimizing your tax situation.

1. Types of Taxes: Taxes can take various forms, including income taxes, capital gains taxes, property taxes, estate taxes, and sales taxes. Each type of tax has its own rules, rates, and implications for your financial situation.

2. Taxation of Different Income Sources: Different sources of income may be subject to different tax rates and treatment. For example, earned income from wages or salaries is typically taxed at ordinary income tax rates, while investment income from dividends and capital gains may be subject to preferential tax rates.

3. Tax Brackets and Marginal Tax Rates: Understanding your tax bracket and marginal tax rates is crucial for optimizing your tax planning. Tax brackets determine the rate at which your income is taxed, with higher incomes generally taxed at higher rates. Marginal tax rates refer to the rate applied to the last dollar of income earned.

4. Timing of Tax Payments: The timing of tax payments can impact your cash flow and overall tax burden. Strategies such as deferring income or accelerating deductions can help manage your tax liabilities effectively.

Tax-Advantaged Accounts

Tax-advantaged accounts are investment vehicles that offer tax benefits or incentives to encourage saving and investing for specific purposes. These accounts can help individuals reduce their current tax liabilities and grow their wealth over time.

1. Retirement Accounts: Retirement accounts, such as 401(k)s, IRAs (Traditional and Roth), and SEP-IRAs, offer tax advantages to individuals saving for retirement. Contributions to these accounts may be tax-deductible (Traditional IRA, SEP-IRA) or made with after-tax dollars (Roth IRA) but grow tax-deferred or tax-free.

2. Health Savings Accounts (HSAs): HSAs are tax-advantaged accounts that allow individuals with high-deductible health insurance plans to save for qualified medical expenses. Contributions to HSAs are tax-deductible, grow tax-free, and withdrawals for qualified medical expenses are tax-free.

3. Education Savings Accounts: Education savings accounts, such as 529 plans and Coverdell Education Savings Accounts (ESAs), offer tax benefits for saving for education expenses. Contributions to these accounts may be tax-deductible (529 plans) or made with after-tax dollars (Coverdell ESAs), and

withdrawals for qualified education expenses are tax-free.

4. Healthcare and Dependent Care Flexible Spending Accounts (FSAs): FSAs allow individuals to set aside pre-tax dollars to pay for qualified medical or dependent care expenses. Contributions to FSAs reduce taxable income, and withdrawals for qualified expenses are tax-free.

Legal Strategies to Minimize Tax Liabilities

In addition to utilizing tax-advantaged accounts, there are various legal strategies individuals can employ to minimize their tax liabilities and optimize their tax situation.

1. Tax Loss Harvesting: Tax loss harvesting involves selling investments that have experienced losses to offset capital gains and reduce taxable income. By strategically harvesting losses, investors can minimize their tax liabilities while maintaining their investment portfolio's overall asset allocation.
2. Charitable Giving: Charitable contributions to qualified organizations may be tax-deductible and can reduce taxable income. Individuals can maximize tax benefits by donating appreciated assets, such as stocks or real estate, directly to charities, thereby avoiding capital gains taxes on the appreciation.

3. Estate Planning: Proper estate planning can help individuals minimize estate taxes and ensure the orderly transfer of wealth to heirs and beneficiaries. Strategies such as gifting, trusts, and life insurance can be used to minimize estate tax liabilities and maximize the transfer of wealth.

4. Business Deductions and Credits: Small business owners and self-employed individuals may be eligible for various deductions and credits to reduce their tax liabilities. Expenses related to business operations, such as office supplies, travel, and marketing, may be deductible, reducing taxable income.

5. Tax-Efficient Investing: Choosing tax-efficient investment strategies, such

as investing in tax-efficient funds, minimizing portfolio turnover, and utilizing tax-loss harvesting techniques, can help minimize tax liabilities and maximize after-tax returns.

CHAPTER FIVE

NETWORKING AND MENTORSHIP

Networking and mentorship are invaluable tools for building wealth and achieving success in both personal and professional endeavors. In this chapter, we'll explore the importance of networking, strategies for building a wealth network, and the benefits of mentorship in guiding your journey towards financial prosperity.

BUILDING A WEALTH NETWORK

1. Importance of Networking:

Networking is the process of establishing and nurturing relationships with individuals who can provide support, guidance, and opportunities for personal and professional growth. In the context of wealth building, networking plays a crucial role in expanding your circle of influence, accessing valuable resources, and unlocking new opportunities.

Networking allows you to:

A. Expand Your Reach: Networking opens doors to new connections and opportunities that you may not have access to otherwise. By building relationships with a diverse range of individuals, you can tap into different networks and perspectives that can enrich your life and career.

B. Exchange Knowledge and Ideas: Networking provides a platform for sharing knowledge, ideas, and experiences with others. Engaging in meaningful conversations and discussions with like-minded individuals can spark creativity, inspire innovation, and accelerate learning and growth.

C. Access Resources and Opportunities: Networking can lead to valuable resources and opportunities, such as job offers, business partnerships, investment opportunities, and mentorship relationships. By cultivating a strong network of contacts, you increase your chances of discovering and capitalizing on new opportunities that align with your goals and aspirations.

2. Finding and Connecting with Influential People:

Building a wealth network involves identifying and connecting with influential individuals who can help you advance your career, grow your business, or achieve your financial goals. Here are some strategies for finding and connecting with influential people:

A. Attend Networking Events: Attend industry conferences, seminars, workshops, and networking events where you can meet and interact with influential individuals in your field or area of interest. Be proactive in initiating conversations and building relationships with key players in your industry.

B. Join Professional Associations: Join professional associations, industry groups, or networking clubs related to your field or interests. These organizations provide opportunities for networking, professional development, and collaboration with other like-minded individuals.

C. Utilize Social Media: Leverage social media platforms such as LinkedIn, Twitter, and Facebook to connect with influential individuals in your industry or niche. Follow thought leaders, engage with their content, and participate in online discussions to establish rapport and build relationships.

D. Seek Introductions: Leverage your existing network to seek introductions to influential individuals who may be able to offer guidance, mentorship, or opportunities for collaboration. Don't be afraid to reach out and request a meeting or conversation to discuss mutual interests and goals.

3. Leveraging Your Network for Opportunities:

Once you've built a wealth network, it's essential to leverage your connections effectively to capitalize on opportunities and achieve your financial objectives. Here are some ways to leverage your network for opportunities:

A. Seek Mentorship: Identify individuals within your network who possess the knowledge, experience, and skills you aspire to develop. Seek mentorship relationships with these individuals to gain valuable insights, guidance, and advice on navigating your career or business endeavors.

B. Explore Collaborative Ventures: Collaborate with individuals in your network on projects, ventures, or initiatives that align with your interests and goals. Pooling resources, expertise, and networks can amplify your impact and create mutually beneficial opportunities for growth and success.

C. Stay Connected and Engaged: Maintain regular communication and engagement with your network to nurture relationships and stay top of mind. Share updates, achievements, and insights with your connections, and offer support and assistance whenever possible. A strong network is built on trust, reciprocity, and mutual support.

MENTORSHIP AND COACHING

Mentorship and coaching are invaluable resources for personal and professional growth, particularly in the realm of financial success. In this chapter, we'll explore the significance of finding the right mentors, strategies for maximizing the benefits of mentorship, and the role of a financial coach in guiding your path to wealth.

Finding the Right Mentors

1. Identifying Potential Mentors:

Finding the right mentors begins with identifying individuals who possess the knowledge, experience, and qualities you admire and aspire to emulate. Mentors can come from various backgrounds and may include:

A. Industry Leaders: Seek out respected leaders and experts in your field or industry who have achieved the level of success you aspire to attain. Look for individuals who have a track record of accomplishment and are willing to share their insights and experiences with others.

B. Personal Connections: Consider reaching out to individuals within your existing network, such as colleagues, peers, or acquaintances, who you admire and respect. Personal connections can provide valuable mentorship opportunities and may be more accessible and relatable than high-profile industry leaders.

C. Professional Organizations: Join professional associations, networking groups, or mentorship programs within your industry or field. These organizations often offer mentorship opportunities, networking events, and resources to connect aspiring professionals with experienced mentors.

2. Building Relationships:

Once you've identified potential mentors, focus on building genuine relationships based on trust, respect, and mutual benefit. Here are some strategies for establishing meaningful connections with mentors:

A. Research and Outreach: Take the time to research your potential mentors and learn about their background, interests, and achievements. Tailor your outreach efforts to demonstrate your genuine interest and appreciation for their work.

B. Offer Value: Approach mentorship as a two-way street and look for ways to offer value to your mentors. Share your skills, expertise, and insights, and be proactive in assisting with their projects or initiatives whenever possible.

C. Be Coachable: Be open-minded, receptive to feedback, and willing to learn from your mentors' experiences and perspectives. Demonstrate humility, curiosity, and a willingness to grow and improve in your personal and professional endeavors.

3. Evaluating Compatibility:

Not every mentorship relationship will be a perfect fit, so it's essential to evaluate compatibility and alignment of goals and values. Consider the following factors when assessing potential mentors:

A. Alignment of Goals: Ensure that your goals and aspirations align with those of your potential mentors. Look for individuals who share similar values, interests, and visions for success.

B. Communication Style: Pay attention to your potential mentors' communication style, personality, and approach to mentoring. Effective mentorship requires clear communication, mutual understanding, and rapport between mentor and mentee.

C. Availability and Commitment: Assess your potential mentors' availability and willingness to invest time and effort in mentorship. Look for individuals who are committed to supporting your growth and development and are available to provide guidance and advice when needed.

How to Get the Most Out of Mentorship

1. Set Clear Goals and Expectations:

Before entering into a mentorship relationship, clarify your goals, objectives, and expectations for mentorship. Define what you hope to achieve through mentorship and communicate your expectations to your mentor.

2. Be Proactive and Prepared:

Take initiative in driving the mentorship process and be proactive in seeking guidance, feedback, and support from your mentor. Come prepared to mentorship meetings with specific questions, topics, or challenges you'd like to discuss.

3. Seek Feedback and Act on Advice:

Be receptive to feedback and constructive criticism from your mentor and take actionable steps to implement their advice and recommendations. Use mentorship as an opportunity for growth, learning, and self-improvement.

4. Stay Committed and Consistent: Maintain regular communication and engagement with your mentor and prioritize mentorship as a key aspect of your personal and professional development. Stay committed to the mentorship process and invest time and effort in building a meaningful relationship with your mentor.

The Role of a Financial Coach

A financial coach plays a vital role in providing guidance, support, and accountability in helping individuals achieve their financial goals and aspirations. Here's how a financial coach can support you on your path to wealth:

1. Goal Setting and Planning:

A financial coach can help you clarify your financial goals, develop a personalized financial plan, and establish actionable steps to achieve your objectives. They can provide expertise and insights into financial planning, budgeting, saving, investing, and debt management.

2. Behavioral Change and Accountability:

A financial coach can help you identify and overcome limiting beliefs, habits, and behaviors that may be hindering your financial success. They can offer encouragement, motivation, and accountability to help you stay on track with your financial goals and make positive changes in your financial behavior.

3. Education and Empowerment:

A financial coach can provide education, resources, and tools to enhance your financial literacy and empower you to make informed decisions about your finances. They can demystify complex financial concepts, clarify your options, and equip you with the knowledge and skills to manage your money effectively.

4. Support and Guidance:

A financial coach serves as a trusted advisor and sounding board for your financial concerns, questions, and challenges. They can offer unbiased guidance, perspective, and support to help you navigate financial decisions, overcome obstacles, and achieve financial peace of mind.

CHAPTER SIX

SCALING AND SUSTAINING WEALTH

Scaling and sustaining wealth require strategic planning, efficient management, and delegation of tasks to maximize productivity and growth. In this chapter, we'll explore the importance of automation and delegation in scaling your wealth, including strategies for automating your finances, delegating tasks to scale faster, and building a reliable team to support your financial endeavors.

AUTOMATION AND DELEGATION

1. Automating Your Finances:

Automation is a powerful tool for streamlining your financial processes, minimizing manual tasks, and optimizing your time and resources. By automating repetitive tasks and financial transactions, you can free up valuable time to focus on higher-value activities and strategic decision-making. Here are some key areas of your finances that you can automate:

A. Bill Payments: Set up automatic bill payments for recurring expenses such as utilities, mortgage or rent payments, insurance premiums, and subscriptions. Automating bill payments helps ensure that you never miss a payment deadline and avoid late fees or penalties.

B. Savings and Investments: Automate contributions to your savings accounts, retirement accounts, and investment portfolios. Set up automatic transfers or direct deposits from your paycheck to your savings or investment accounts to ensure consistent savings and investment contributions over time.

C. Budgeting and Expense Tracking: Use budgeting and expense tracking apps or software to automate the process of categorizing and tracking your expenses. These tools can help you monitor your spending habits, identify areas for cost savings, and stay within your budget limits.

D. Tax Payments and Filings: Automate tax payments, filings, and compliance tasks to ensure timely and accurate submission of your tax obligations. Use tax preparation software or hire a tax professional to automate tax calculations, filings, and payments, reducing the risk of errors and penalties.

2. Delegating Tasks to Scale Faster: Delegation is essential for scaling your wealth and expanding your financial endeavors beyond your individual capacity. By delegating tasks to capable team members or professionals, you can leverage their expertise, skills, and resources to accelerate growth and achieve your financial goals more efficiently. Here are some tasks you can consider delegating to scale faster:

A. Administrative Tasks: Delegate administrative tasks such as bookkeeping, data entry, scheduling, and correspondence to administrative assistants or virtual assistants. Outsourcing routine administrative tasks frees up your time to focus on strategic priorities and high-impact activities.

B. Investment Management: Consider delegating investment management tasks such as portfolio construction, asset allocation, and investment research to financial advisors or investment professionals. Outsourcing investment management allows you to benefit from expert guidance and decision-making while freeing up time to focus on other aspects of your wealth-building strategy.

C. Business Operations: Delegate operational tasks such as inventory management, customer service, marketing, and sales to employees or contractors. By building a capable team and delegating operational responsibilities, you can scale your business operations more effectively and focus on strategic growth initiatives.

D. Legal and Compliance Matters: Delegate legal and compliance tasks such as contract negotiations, regulatory compliance, and risk management to legal professionals or compliance officers. Outsourcing legal and compliance matters ensures that your business operations are conducted in accordance with applicable laws and regulations, reducing the risk of legal issues or penalties.

3. Building a Reliable Team:

Building a reliable team is essential for sustaining wealth and achieving long-term success in your financial endeavors. A reliable team consists of individuals who share your vision, values, and commitment to excellence and can support you in achieving your goals. Here are some key considerations for building a reliable team:

A. Recruitment and Selection: Identify talented individuals with the skills, experience, and cultural fit to contribute to your team's success. Use a rigorous recruitment and selection process to attract top talent and ensure alignment with your organization's values and objectives.

B. Training and Development: Invest in training and development programs to equip your team members with the knowledge, skills, and resources they need to excel in their roles. Provide ongoing coaching, mentoring, and feedback to support their professional growth and development.

C. Communication and Collaboration: Foster open communication and collaboration among team members to promote transparency, trust, and teamwork. Encourage regular team meetings, brainstorming sessions, and feedback mechanisms to facilitate communication and collaboration across your organization.

D. Recognition and Rewards: Recognize and reward team members for their contributions, achievements, and excellence. Implement reward and recognition programs to acknowledge outstanding performance, incentivize high performance, and reinforce desired behaviors and outcomes.

SUSTAINING WEALTH

Sustaining wealth is as crucial as building it. It involves maintaining financial discipline, diversifying income streams, and preparing for market downturns to ensure long-term financial stability and prosperity. In this section, we'll delve into these essential aspects of wealth sustainability and explore practical strategies for implementing them effectively.

Maintaining Financial Discipline

Financial discipline is the foundation of long-term wealth sustainability. It involves managing your finances responsibly, adhering to a budget, and making informed decisions about saving, spending, and investing. Here's why maintaining financial discipline is vital:

1. Budgeting: Creating and sticking to a budget is essential for maintaining financial discipline. A budget helps you track your income and expenses, identify areas for cost-cutting or savings,

and ensure that you're living within your means.

2. Saving and Investing: Practicing regular saving and investing habits is key to building wealth over time. Allocate a portion of your income towards savings and investments, and automate contributions to retirement accounts, investment portfolios, and emergency funds.

3. Avoiding Debt: Minimizing debt and managing debt responsibly is critical for maintaining financial discipline. Avoid high-interest consumer debt, such as credit card debt, and focus on paying off existing debts to free up cash flow and reduce financial stress.

4. Living Below Your Means: Adopting a frugal lifestyle and living below your means allows you to save and invest more aggressively, build wealth faster, and achieve financial independence sooner. Prioritize needs over wants, practice mindful spending, and avoid unnecessary expenses.

Diversifying Income Streams

Diversifying income streams is essential for mitigating risk, increasing resilience, and ensuring financial stability in the face of economic uncertainty. Relying on a single source of income leaves you vulnerable to unexpected changes or disruptions in the economy or job market. Here's why diversifying income streams is crucial:

1. Risk Mitigation: Diversifying income streams helps spread risk across multiple sources, reducing dependence on any single source of income. If one income stream is affected by economic downturns or industry-specific challenges, other income streams can provide a buffer and support your financial stability.

2. Income Stability: Diversified income streams provide more stable and predictable cash flow, even during periods of economic volatility. Different income sources may have varying cycles or seasons, balancing out fluctuations and ensuring a steady stream of income throughout the year.

3. Expanding Opportunities: Diversifying income streams opens up new opportunities for generating revenue and expanding your earning potential. Explore different avenues for generating income, such as side hustles, freelancing, rental properties, investments, or passive income streams.

4. Flexibility and Adaptability: Diversified income streams offer flexibility and adaptability in response to changing market conditions or personal circumstances. If one income stream becomes less profitable or relevant, you can pivot to focus on other income sources that offer better opportunities for growth and success.

Preparing for Market Downturns

Market downturns are inevitable and can have a significant impact on your financial well-being if you're not prepared. Whether it's a recession, stock market crash, or industry downturn, being proactive and resilient in the face of market downturns is essential for sustaining wealth. Here's how to prepare for market downturns effectively:

1. Emergency Fund: Maintain an emergency fund with sufficient savings to cover essential expenses for three to six months or more. An emergency fund provides a financial safety net during periods of job loss, income reduction, or unexpected expenses, allowing you to weather temporary financial setbacks

without resorting to debt or liquidating investments.

2. Asset Allocation: Review and adjust your investment portfolio's asset allocation to ensure it's aligned with your risk tolerance, investment objectives, and time horizon. Diversify your investments across different asset classes, industries, and geographic regions to minimize exposure to specific risks and market downturns.

3. Long-Term Perspective: Maintain a long-term perspective and avoid making impulsive investment decisions based on short-term market fluctuations or fear-driven emotions. Stay focused on your investment goals, stick to your investment strategy, and use market

downturns as buying opportunities to acquire quality assets at discounted prices.

4. Continuous Learning: Stay informed about economic trends, market developments, and investment strategies through continuous learning and education. Keep abreast of changes in the financial markets, seek advice from trusted financial professionals, and remain flexible and adaptable in your investment approach.

GIVING BACK

Giving back through philanthropy is not only a noble endeavor but also a strategic way to increase wealth, create a positive impact on society, and leave a lasting legacy. In this section, we'll explore the importance of philanthropy, how giving back can increase wealth, and the significance of creating a legacy through charitable acts.

The Importance of Philanthropy

1. Social Impact: Philanthropy plays a crucial role in addressing social issues, supporting underserved communities, and driving positive change in society. By donating time, money, or resources to charitable causes, philanthropists can make a tangible difference in the lives of individuals and communities in need.

2. Personal Fulfillment: Engaging in philanthropy can provide a sense of purpose, fulfillment, and satisfaction derived from making a meaningful contribution to the greater good. Giving

back allows individuals to connect with causes they're passionate about, align their values with their actions, and experience the joy of giving.

3. Community Engagement: Philanthropy fosters community engagement, collaboration, and social cohesion by bringing together individuals, businesses, and organizations to address common challenges and work towards shared goals. By supporting local initiatives and community-based organizations, philanthropists can strengthen the fabric of their communities and foster a sense of belonging and solidarity.

4. Leadership and Influence: Philanthropy provides an opportunity

for individuals to exercise leadership, influence, and stewardship in addressing pressing societal issues and driving positive change. By leveraging their resources, networks, and expertise, philanthropists can inspire others to join their cause, mobilize collective action, and effect systemic change.

How Giving Back Can Increase Wealth

1. Wealth Maximization: Contrary to popular belief, philanthropy can be a strategic tool for wealth maximization and financial success. By giving back to charitable causes, individuals can enhance their reputation, build goodwill, and attract new opportunities

for business, career advancement, and personal growth.

2. Networking and Relationships: Engaging in philanthropy provides opportunities to network with like-minded individuals, influential leaders, and potential collaborators or partners. Building relationships through philanthropic activities can open doors to new opportunities, referrals, and connections that can ultimately contribute to wealth creation and expansion.

3. Brand Enhancement: For businesses and entrepreneurs, corporate philanthropy can enhance brand reputation, customer loyalty, and employee morale. By demonstrating a

commitment to social responsibility and giving back to the community, companies can differentiate themselves in the marketplace, attract socially conscious consumers, and drive positive brand perception and loyalty.

4. Tax Benefits: Philanthropy offers significant tax benefits for individuals and businesses, including charitable tax deductions, exemptions, and credits. By donating to qualified charitable organizations, philanthropists can reduce their taxable income, lower their tax liabilities, and maximize their after-tax returns, effectively increasing their net worth and wealth accumulation.

Creating a Legacy

1. Generational Impact: Philanthropy allows individuals to create a lasting legacy that extends beyond their lifetime, leaving a positive impact on future generations. By supporting causes they care about and establishing charitable foundations or endowments, philanthropists can ensure that their values, beliefs, and vision for a better world endure for years to come.

2. Inspiring Others: Philanthropy serves as a powerful example of leadership, generosity, and social responsibility, inspiring others to follow suit and contribute to meaningful causes. By sharing their philanthropic journey, stories, and successes,

philanthropists can motivate and empower others to make a difference in their own communities and spheres of influence.

3. Personal Reflection and Growth: Engaging in philanthropy provides opportunities for personal reflection, growth, and self-discovery. By examining their values, priorities, and life purpose, philanthropists can gain a deeper understanding of themselves and their place in the world, leading to personal fulfillment, growth, and transformation.

4. Long-Term Sustainability: Philanthropy promotes long-term sustainability and resilience by investing in solutions that address root causes,

build capacity, and create lasting change. By supporting sustainable development projects, education initiatives, and social entrepreneurship ventures, philanthropists can contribute to building a more equitable, inclusive, and sustainable future for all.

THE END

www.ingramcontent.com/pod-product-compliance
Lightning Source LLC
Chambersburg PA
CBHW050216230526
45470CB00001B/415